Dedication

This book is dedicated to my parents, John and Catherine Moran, who gave me a strong core of moral values.

It is also dedicated to my wife, Lili who encouraged me to make this book a reality and challenges me to be the best I can be in all I do.

Disclaimer

This book is for general educational purposes, however all concepts and ideas herein should be thoroughly researched and verified prior to application. Any action on the part of the reader based in whole or in part on the information contained herein should be understood to be made solely at the discretion of the reader. It should be understood that each individual's personal financial needs differ and there is no single formula or set of ideas that is right for everyone. It is the responsibility of the reader to determine whether any of the ideas herein are suitable for the reader's personal needs and reader takes all personal responsibility for any action taken.

This book is presented solely for educational and entertainment purposes. The author and publisher are not offering it as legal, accounting, or other professional services advice. While best efforts have been used in preparing this book, the author and publisher make no representations or warranties of any kind and assume no liabilities of any kind with respect to the accuracy or completeness of the contents and specifically disclaim any implied warranties of merchantability or fitness of use for a particular purpose. Neither the author nor the publisher shall be held liable or responsible to any person or entity with respect to any loss or incidental or consequential damages caused, or alleged to have been caused, directly or indirectly, by the information contained herein. No warranty may be created or extended. Every person is different and the advice and strategies contained herein may not be suitable for your situation. You should seek the services of a competent professional before beginning any improvement program.

Although the author and publisher have made every effort to ensure that the information in this book was correct at press time, the author and publisher do not assume and hereby disclaim any liability to any party for any loss, damage, or disruption caused by errors or omissions, whether such errors or omissions result from negligence, accident, or any other cause.

TABLE OF CONTENTS

SAVING FOR THE FUTURE AND WEALTH DEVELOPMENT

A penny here, and a dollar there, placed at interest, goes on accumulating, and in this way the desired result is attained. It requires some training, perhaps, to accomplish this economy, but when once used to it, you will find there is more satisfaction in rational saving than in irrational spending. ~ *The Art of Money Getting, by P. T. Barnum*

Introduction

When I started college, my dad gave me his 6 year old Honda Civic with 100,000 plus miles on it. One of the first things I had to do was change out the spark plugs. I asked my dad if he could help me, but he said that I could figure it out. Without the benefit of the internet and YouTube back in the early 90's, I turned to the owner's manual. It essentially told me to remove the old plugs and put new ones in. After about an hour, I walked into the house, proud of myself and announced that I successfully changed the spark plugs. With that, my father asked: "Did you gap the spark plugs?" My response was, "What the heck does that mean?"

The moral of the story is I didn't know what I didn't know! Unless you know what you don't know, you are at a big disadvantage. You don't know where to start, or worse yet, you get it wrong.

I had never heard of gapping spark plugs, so how could I possibly have been expected to do it? When it comes to finances, do you sometimes feel like you don't know what it is you need to do? If only you knew the rules, or where to start, then you would have a much better chance of getting the job done right.

Having felt lost myself at one point, I wanted to put together a guide to help people through the confusing world of finances. It's much easier when you know what you need to do. The question is: how do you know what you don't know?

This book will set out a good foundation to get you on your way. With the benefit of the internet at your fingertips, you should be able to take the concepts here and dig deeper to develop your plan. If you still struggle, it may be time to get a good financial coach to help you along the way.

I have set this book up in what I hope is a simple, orderly step by step process for wealth accumulation and savings.

Not having a plan for your financial future is like throwing a Hail Mary pass and hoping to win in the end. The chances of success are poor.

CHAPTER 1

SPENDING AND SAVING

The Golden Rule: Debt destroys financial freedom

Nothing is more damaging to a successful financial future than amassing debt. When you purchase things that you do not have the money to pay for, money that you would otherwise save goes to someone else. On top of paying back the debt, you also pay interest, which can, in some cases be equal to or even more than the amount you originally borrowed.

There is no such thing as a sound financial plan that involves amassing considerable debt - especially high interest debt like credit cards. This chapter will lay out the steps to best get your financial situation in order and achieve freedom from debt. These steps will apply to most people, but everyone's situation is different. You need to adjust your plan to best fit your needs. Remember, there is no substitute for a sound financial plan when it comes to establishing a secure financial future. The future starts now.

Keeping Track of Spending

With anything in life, you can't be successful unless you have a plan. Finance is no different. How can you tell if you reached a goal, if you haven't set one? How do you know if you saved enough money or spent too much?

According to a recent article on Market Watch a survey of 750 investors revealed that 89% were confident their investing strategy would result in them achieving their goals for retirement. Over 70% of them admitted that they have a weak level of investment knowledge and greater than 50% noted they do not have a financial plan with about 45% saying they have not defined clear financial goals. (Coombes, 2013)

If people don't have a plan, how do they expect to measure their success? Isn't that like setting out on a cross country road trip without a GPS, a map or an address of your final destination?

This whole process of financial goal setting includes making a budget. Start by writing down your weekly or monthly take home pay in one column and all of your expenses in another. Compare the two. Which column is greater, income or expenses? If the expenses are larger, or even if they are smaller, but close to income, then spending cuts need to happen.

Breaking even isn't good enough; you need a plan that will leave you enough extra money to cover the additional savings and emergencies that life throws your way. How much do you need? Read on and you will get a better idea, but as with any decisions, everyone will have a different answer as to what fits them best.

Remember each person's definition of "enough money" or being wealthy is different. Just like someone who makes $40,000 a year would say that making $80,000 is a lot of money, a person who is making $500,000 would think $250,000 isn't enough.

If you aren't good at keeping track of your spending yourself, consider getting a program like Quicken, or going online to Mint.com or another similar site that will help aggregate all your accounts and let you keep track of your money in a simple to follow manner. If you are wealthy, it might make sense to hire a trustworthy, credentialed person to help you in this regard.

Paying off Debt

One of the keys to financial freedom is to amass wealth while keeping costs and debt to a minimum. If you happened to rack up some credit card debt, it is important to pay this down; either in conjunction with saving or prior to saving, depending on the cost (aka interest rate) of the debt. Clearly if your credit card charges you 18% or more in interest and you can't get anywhere near that in an investment, you should pay off the credit card debt first.

Causes of debt

It is also important to understand what it was that got you into debt in the first place, so that it can be avoided in the future. We will discuss some of the causes and then a plan for paying down the debt.

Did you amass the debt because you fell on hard times and you had no safety net to pay your bills and your credit cards were the only way to stay afloat while the income was not coming in the door? If this is the case, the section on creating a Rainy Day Fund below is one you will appreciate. Sometimes we just have to make ends meet, but if you find that you are tapping into the credit cards over and over, then you will need to figure out how to increase your income and/or lower your expenses.

Another cause of increased debt is poor spending habits. Do you enjoy going on shopping sprees but when the bills come in you are shocked at what you owe? If this is what caused your debt, then you want to consider cutting up your credit cards. If you continue your excess spending behavior, you will find that you fall deeper and deeper in debt, because for every dollar you are paying off, you seem to add at least another dollar, or more, to your balance. This is a dangerous cycle to get into, because it is often difficult to get out of.

Debt solutions

A feasible option might be to take a certain amount of cash from your budget and use that for discretionary spending. When you have no money left, then your spending for the month is over. This is a good way to put discipline in your spending. Remember to allocate only an amount you can truly afford to spend and do not go over that amount. No credit cards!

Consider, also, when you pick something up in a store; ask yourself "Is this something I really need?" If the answer is an honest no, then don't get it.

Another solution could be to tell yourself that for each new thing you buy, you need to sell something else you own to help pay for it (and to keep your life from being cluttered). For example, if you have a lot of clothing, maybe you need to sell the items you haven't worn on eBay or somewhere else. Maybe you choose to donate them to charity, so you can get a tax deduction and you can spend the tax deduction amount.

Paying off the debt you have

Now that you have figured out what is causing the debt, whether a one-time tough experience that will not repeat or a lifestyle change as discussed above, you can focus on the pay-off plan.

Credit card debt typically carries with it the highest interest rates out there. Some cards carry rates as high as 18-21% or more. You might find that some of your credit card statements have a section that tells you that if you make the minimum payment, it will take you years to pay off the debt and cost you many times more than what you purchased.   A good rule for those that if you carry a balance: do not put anything on the card that will be used up before you pay for it, like gas, meals, etc.

When you are undertaking a plan to pay off your credit card debt, first look at all the credit cards on which you are carrying balances from month to month. Organize them by interest rate and by balance. Are there any with a small balance you could pay off right away, while still paying at least the minimum on all the others? If so, pay that off and then look at the highest interest rate cards and pay the most on those and the least on the lowest rate cards. If you have more than 2-3 credit cards, ask yourself why you have so many and whether you should have them in the first place. Keep in mind that you don't want to close a bunch of accounts at once, nor do you want to close the account you have had the longest, because this could hurt your credit rating, but consider whether there are a few you can pay off and close over the course of 6 months to a year. Your credit rating is vital if you plan to seek credit in the future. If you have poor credit it is unlikely that you will be extended credit in the future for good uses (such as buying a house, car or business). If you do find someone willing to extended credit to you when you have poor credit, you will find that the interest rate you get will be higher than your friends that have good credit. This means you end up paying more for items than others do, or worse, you get turned down for credit. If you are turned down, you have to put your financial decisions on hold. That can be a major setback.

If you have a good credit rating and you know you aren't going to be able to pay your balances in a month or two, consider getting a low introductory card and transferring your balances to that card. Keep in mind that there is usually a fee associated with making that transfer, so be sure that fee is lower than the interest you would be paying by keeping it on the card you have already. If you are carrying a balance of $1,000 or more, you could potentially save yourself considerable money by transferring that from a high rate credit card to a 1.5% or even a 0% rate card. Just make sure you understand the terms of the new card agreement. Does it say you get that low rate for the introductory period and then it goes up to the prevailing rate? If it does, you may want to transfer the balance again when you get to the end of that period. Some cards might say that they accrue the interest and if you don't pay the balance off before the end of the period, they will charge you additional interest or fees. The point here is to make sure you know what you are agreeing to, just like you should in any other transaction.

Remember, a sound plan and keeping debt to a minimum are the foundation of a secure financial future. Use the suggestions in this book to help put your plan together.

CHAPTER 2

RETIREMENT

Are you saving enough for retirement?

I bet you are wondering why retirement is chapter 2, when retirement is so far away if you are just starting out. Keep reading and it will become clear that this is not in the wrong place.

About a year ago, I was away on a business trip and the hotel left me a copy of USA Today. On the cover was a headline noting that more than half of Americans nearing retirement age have under $25,000 saved for retirement.

Are you one of these people, or are you younger, but have no plan in place to put yourself in a better financial situation than the average American?

Do a quick internet search, or even consider your own personal situation. How much do you think the cost of living is in the US on an annual basis? Is it unreasonable to think that rent, food and a few essentials would cost less than $15,000 - $20,000 per year? If that's the case, then you are out of money in less than two years if you only save $25,000 total. What are you going to do after that?

You may say that you plan to work through retirement and that may work, but what if you aren't healthy enough to work? What if you want to take a vacation one year or perhaps buy a car?

I am talking about retirement, because it is one of the most overlooked areas of finance and typically, people have no plan or an insufficient one if they have one at all. If you are young, you might think you have plenty of time. If you are closer to retirement, you may think it is too late. You would be wrong on both counts.

When I graduated from college, I read an article that demonstrated that if you save $5,000 a year from age 25 to age 35 and then didn't save another dollar until age 60, you would have more money saved than someone who put $5,000 away every single year from age 35 to age 60.

In other words, your $55,000 investment between age 25-35 will grow to be more money than saving $130,000 from the age of 35 – 60. How is that possible? The answer is compound interest.

If you were to use an annual rate of return of 8% (meaning you earn 8% per year) on your money you would have roughly $615,000 at age 60 under the first plan and $430,000 with the second plan.

Imagine if you saved the $5,000 each and every year from age 25-60? You can see where you might have a comfortable retirement.

If you are already 35 or older, remember it isn't too late. Start putting as much money away as you can.

Even if you save $5,000 a year for the next 10 years, assuming the same 8% return on your money, you would have $78,000 saved, which is much more than the average person has saved. I would still argue that $78,000 will not be enough, but it's a much better situation to be in than having $25,000.

Where to put your money

Hopefully by now you are convinced that you need to save for retirement. So where do you put your money?

If you have a company sponsored 401(k) plan, the answer is to start there. If you don't, then you will want to get an Individual Retirement Account (IRA). An IRA is similar to a 401(k) plan, in that both allow you to save for retirement in such a way that will save you taxes. A 401(k) is better, however, because it allows you to save more.

If you need an IRA, most major brokerage companies as well as your bank can help you set up an IRA and typically they can even do an electronic transfer from your checking or savings account.

Keep in mind that there are annual limits to the amount you are allowed to save in a 401(k) or IRA, so don't put more than you are permitted to. Having said that, if you have a company sponsored plan and they provide a matching contribution, be sure to contribute at least as much as they are going to match or you are leaving free money on the table. For example, some companies will make a contribution to your account matching the first 6% of your salary with 50 cents per dollar you contribute. So if you make $100,000 and you put $6,000 (or 6%) into your 401(k) they will put an additional 3% in there for you. That means you will have $9,000 saved when you only put in $6,000. That is a great deal.

Before you decide to put money into another type of account that doesn't have a tax advantage, make sure you have maximized your contribution to the plan you have at work or your IRA.

There are some people that might tell you that occasionally there is a better place to save than a retirement plan, but generally speaking that isn't the case. Do a bit of research to decide for yourself, but in most cases, a retirement plan is a great idea.

Traditional vs. Roth Account?

When it comes to retirement accounts, there are two types, the traditional and the Roth plan. You might have heard the term IRA or Roth IRA. While both are designed for retirement savings, the tax consequences are different with each. Some companies are even setting up Roth 401(k) plans as well as traditional. For simplicity, I will use the term IRA to mean either an IRA or a 401(k). If you have a 401(k) instead of an IRA, the concept is the same and you can just substitute the term 401(k) in your mind where I write IRA.

Let's define each and then we can talk about the differences. You can then choose which plan works best for you, though I definitely have a bias toward the traditional account.

A traditional IRA is one in which you put money into a qualified account and you are given a tax deduction for that contribution, almost as if you did not earn that income. Said differently, you are saving pre-tax money. By way of example, if you make $50,000 and you put $5,000 into a traditional IRA, when you file your tax return you will be reporting $45,000 as your wages instead of $50,000. As a result of this deduction, you are paying less tax for the year than you would have if you didn't put this money away. Assuming you are in the 15% tax bracket, you save $750 a year in taxes.

The tradeoff here is that when you retire, you will have to pay taxes on this money when you take it out. You save $750 now, but pay tax on it in retirement. Isn't that like buying something now and paying for it later? That is definitely a good deal, considering you aren't going to have to pay interest on it when you withdraw later. The only argument I have heard against this is if you are in the 15% tax bracket, for instance, now and you believe that in retirement you will be in a higher tax bracket, such that paying the tax now at 15% will be less money than paying say 27% on that money when you retire. That is a mathematical equation that you can figure out, but in most cases less tax now is going to be the better option. If you think it's not the better option, consider the Roth IRA.

The Roth IRA works a little differently. Instead of putting away pre-tax money and paying tax when you retire, the plan is set up so you put away money after tax, but then when you retire, you can withdraw that money, including earnings without paying tax on it. Using the same example as above, you pay tax on the full $50,000 per year, so you pay $750 more in taxes in the current year, but when you retire and take the money out, you will not pay tax on it.

Which is a better deal for you, a Roth or traditional?

Conventional wisdom would tell you that if you expect your tax rate to be higher when you retire, then go with the Roth, but if you expect it to be lower, go with traditional.

I believe it is better to stick with the traditional IRA, because you save money today. What happens if down the line the government believes they need more money? They could potentially take away some or all of the benefits of the Roth IRA and then you end up having paid taxes now (when you earn the money) and you get less of a benefit later.   With the traditional IRA you get the benefit now.

Keep in mind that there is no single best investment strategy and this is just one person's opinion. Everyone should analyze their own facts and circumstances to see what fits their situation best.

Researching the arguments on both sides and truly understanding the benefits of both is essential.

Grow your contributions painlessly

When you start out your career, you have a small amount of disposable income, so it is difficult to max out your contribution to your retirement account. When I started out, I made about $25,000 a year, so putting away $14,000 plus per year wasn't feasible. As the years went by, I was getting annual raises of maybe 4-6%, so I raised my contribution to my 401(k) by 3-5%. I did that every year until I was putting in the maximum allowed amount. Never once did I receive less take home pay, because I just put in more as I made more. This is the painless way to save. Start small and build.

Never take an early withdrawal or loan from your Retirement Account

Remember, there is an exception to every rule, but unless you have no other option, do not take money from your retirement account before you reach retirement age. The key here is _before_ retirement age.

There are two ways you can take money out early. One is a simple withdrawal and the other is to borrow from your account. Neither is a good option, but the withdrawal is the worst option. If you withdraw, you pay tax on the amount you withdrew plus you pay a 20% penalty on that amount. That makes the money very expensive. If you think of the 20% penalty as being interest, then you just lost 20% of your investment, plus the tax on that money when it comes out.

The second way you can take an early withdrawal is, if you have a qualifying reason, you may be able to borrow from your retirement account, but this too can be quite costly.

Some people say borrowing from your retirement account is like borrowing from yourself. They will argue that you take money out and then you pay it back with interest, so you are getting the money back into your account. The question is whether or not that is accurate.

Let's use an example again here. Assume that you normally put $6,000 a year or $500 a month into your retirement account. You decide that you have a reason to borrow money from your account and it is a qualifying reason, so you take out $12,000 in the current year to use for that reason. Assume that your plan is giving you 2 years to pay this back and the interest rate is 4%. Basically you will be paying $521 a month back to your plan over the course of the next two years to pay back this loan. Assume that you could have otherwise borrowed the $12,000 from a bank at a 5% interest rate, so you would owe $526 a month. It sounds like borrowing from your retirement account is a better deal right? Wrong!

You might say that saving $5 per month or $120 total on your loan makes it a better deal to borrow from your retirement account, but let's assume that during that time, if you instead left the money in your account, and the market rose such that the investments that you would have had that $12,000 in have a 10% increase in value. Guess what? Your $12,000 wasn't in those investments, so you lost out on that gain. This means you lost the opportunity to make a $1,200 return on your investment, because your money wasn't there. Saving $120 just cost you $1,200.

The other thing to consider is whether you will be paying off the amount in the retirement account while continuing to invest the $500 a month you were saving before you borrowed. This isn't always the case, because most people will just pay off the loan and only start contributing again after they have paid off the loan, so now they have missed out on two years of adding to their account.

Based on the potential for significant financial losses explained above, it's better to borrow elsewhere and let your retirement account continue to grow.

Don't count on Social Security

We all hope that when we get to retirement age, the government checks will come rolling in. This is like the childhood story of the ant and the grasshopper. If you recall, the ant was storing up for winter (retirement) and the grasshopper was just going on his merry way, enjoying the summer weather. When winter came, the grasshopper was in serious trouble. He didn't have anything stored up for the lean times and ended up in a terrible place. Don't be the grasshopper.

While ideally, Social Security would be there to help, it would simply be a crutch for a bleeding leg. It helps, but it isn't enough.

If the 2013 projections by the Congressional Budget Office are to be believed - and I think they should be – the Social Security system (the system) is not sustainable and will go bankrupt. As our population ages and people live longer, we are seeing a lot more people drawing on Social Security. Because most families have the average 2.5 children, there is a gap of people in the workforce and not nearly as many paying into the system.

Don't be fooled into believing that the money coming out of your paycheck is going into some special account for you. There is no such account and the money is just not there, except for current funds coming in from the paychecks of those working. That means that over time, there is no way to sustain this program on its own. What will that mean for you? Either the government will have to discontinue the program, raise the age of eligibility, tax people working at a higher rate to make up the difference or some combination of the above.

If you save for your retirement, then you will be like the ant in the children's story, and you will not have to worry about the cold winter, or whether a Social Security check will be there when you retire. Better to be safe than sorry, so save what you can, then save some more!

CHAPTER 3

<u>RAINY DAY FUND</u>

Everyone needs a rainy day fund

The idea of a rainy day fund is to have money set aside in case of an emergency. What if your car breaks down or you lose your job, etc.? Ideally you should be building your rainy day fund concurrently with your retirement account. A good rule of thumb is to save 3-6 months' worth of expenses into an account that can be accessed in case of an emergency.

To determine how much you need for your fund, calculate the cost of car payments, rent or mortgage, utilities and all other necessary expenses and start a fund to cover these expenses if your current income is not available to do so.

Be sure to consider expenses like the cost of looking for a new job, such as sending out resumes, going on interviews, buying a new suit or other clothing for interview purposes.   In addition, look for ways to reduce expenses so that you become accustomed to living on less and you can make an easier transition if you find yourself without your regular source of income for a period of time.

How can you save 6 months' worth of living expenses? It takes a disciplined approach, but there are simple things you can do daily to start saving. Below is a list of easy tricks to help cut your budget.

Pay yourself first: We all pay our rent/mortgage, utility bills, and all the other essentials and then we look to see what's left.   What about flipping that logic upside down and looking at your budget and "paying" your savings as if it is a bill? You might calculate that you can put away $100 a week, or maybe $500 a month or more. Pay that into a savings account or investment as though you were paying a bill. Don't touch this money, because it's "gone" to pay that hypothetical bill. Only use it in the case of a true emergency where you can't otherwise make payments with regular income.

Pack your lunch: If you make a sandwich for lunch a few times a week instead of going out to lunch, you can save $10-30 plus per week. Save that money in your rainy day fund.

Skip the movie: If you typically go to the movies weekly or regularly, watch one on DVD and put that savings away.

Cook at home: Going out to dinner is fun and worth doing from time to time, but making dinner at home can also be fun and saves a lot of money. Not a good cook? These days, grocery stores sell pre-made meals, such as cooked whole chicken, sides and salads etc. The price to feed a family of 4 this way is often cheaper than 1 person's meal at a reasonably priced chain restaurant.

Don't spend your change: Bank of America has a program called "Keep the Change". I practice that in my daily life. I buy everything with dollars and put the change in a container at home. I then add it up and deposit $50-$100 into savings after a few months' time.

Miscellaneous: Movies not your thing? Maybe you go out for ice cream, buy the newspaper or an expensive drink at your favorite coffee shop every day or have some other indulgence. Try making them at home to save money. Use your imagination and consider whether what you are spending your money on is really adding value to your life compared to the sense of security you will have when you fully fund your rainy day account.

When I was a boy, my mom had a can on top of the washing machine. For every load of laundry she did, she deposited fifty cents and the same for every time she used the dryer. That money was our vacation fund and believe me, with a family of 4 children, there was enough laundry in a week to fund a conservative family vacation. In today's dollars, you might want to put $1 per wash or dry. You decide, but stick with it.

Track your spending: You might think a dollar here for a soda in the vending machine, or $5 there for a coffee isn't much, but if you add it up, you may be surprised how much you are spending and how little value you actually get for that money. Have you ever looked at your credit card statement and were shocked by the balance? I think we all have. Then you go down the itemized list and the $50 at one store and $75 at another and so on adds up to $500, $1,000 or maybe more in a month. Keeping track as you go along will help you see the $50 and $75 before it becomes $1,000 or more and will allow you to cut back to keep the spending in check. I personally use Mint.com but maybe you would use Quicken, a simple spreadsheet, or even a notebook or some other method of tracking your spending.

Is it worth it?: When you go shopping at the mall or your favorite variety store, do you find that you go in for one item and come out with a bunch of things you didn't plan to buy? It's really easy to fall into this trap. Before you pick up that great novelty T Shirt, or that new gadget that you are sure you will find a use for, ask yourself one of the following questions: "Do I really need this?" or "Will I really use this?". If you can honestly say yes, then go for it, but if there is even a little doubt, put it back. This is not to say that you never buy the item, but give it a week or two and if you find you can easily live without it, you just saved money. If you can't go on for another moment without it, go back and buy that blanket with sleeves or fancy bottle opener you just can't live without.

It's on sale! : There is a saying that goes something like this: "A man will pay $10 for a $5 item he needs. A woman will spend $5 for a $10 item she doesn't need." If you find any truth in that statement, regardless of your gender, which one do you think is worse? I would argue that both are a waste of money and each person could have saved $5. Try to steer clear of the mentality that something is worth paying extra for just because it's convenient. With internet shopping it's always easy to get that $5 item without overpaying. Similarly, as I noted in the above section, if it isn't something you will use, then it is a complete waste of money, so don't get it. Save that money in your rainy day fund.

Use your imagination, these are just a few ideas, but the possibilities are endless for saving. Have fun with it.

CHAPTER 4

BUYING A CAR

"The cheapest car you will ever own is the one you already have" – Unknown

Let's start out by saying, if you are a millionaire buy any car you want and move on to the next chapter. For the rest of us, a poor car buying decision can completely derail any financial plan.

Buying more than you can afford

My brother has run a call center with hundreds of employees for many years. What he finds all too often is that his employees, who might make $10 per hour and with commission on sales could bump that up to $20 often drive expensive cars like BMW's and Mercedes Benz's. We are talking cars that cost more than their annual salary.

He questioned many of them about their choice in cars and they simply shrug it off saying that they live with their parents, so a big car payment is really no big deal. Well, it actually is, because they are spending a full year's salary on one item over the next 3-5 years. That's equivalent to paying 20-35% of their income on something that will be worth so much less when you are done paying for it.   When you are making payments of $500 or more per month on a car, you are spending a large amount of cash (that you can otherwise save) on an asset that is continually depreciating. Not a wise move.

A friend of mine bought a BMW 330 series in 2003. He told me that it was a great investment, because BMW's hold their value really well. When he told me the car cost $54,000 I almost fell on the floor. Now this guy has a decent job and he is otherwise good with his money, so this wasn't completely out of the realm of his affordability, but I challenged the premise that the car would hold that kind of value. Fast forward about three to four years and he decided he would trade his BMW in for a newer model. After going to several dealerships he was offered at most $25,000 for his car. Most of us would say that's a great amount, but when you consider this means the car lost $29,000 of its initial value, that is a lot of money that just disappeared. By comparison, I bought a new Nissan Xterra in 2005 for only $22,000, so even if my car would become totally worthless in four years, I would have lost much less than he did on his car.

In 2011, I sold my Xterra, a 6 year old vehicle and I got $13,000. The moral of the story is we both lost half the value of what we paid for the car in about 5 years or so. The more you pay for the car, the more you lose. I am not even counting interest on the loans in the calculations above, but that means it's even more expensive.

Term of car loan

I know a lot of people that concern themselves only with the monthly payment when it comes to buying a car.   Dealers know this and therefore make it sound like a great deal to tell you "It's only $299 per month", or whatever the amount comes out to. Beware when you hear this. What they aren't telling you is that you will be paying $299 a month for the next five years. So what, you say? Well, any time you buy a car there is a magic thing that happens right around 3 to 3.5 years out on a five year loan: The amount you owe on the car becomes more than the car is actually worth, because the book value of the car has dropped so significantly.   That means if the car is stolen or totaled in an accident, you will have to pull additional cash out of your pocket just to get to even. If you decide to trade the car in at that point, the same thing happens; you are essentially in the hole.   The term for this is "upside down on your loan".

Going back to the $299/month example above, I put together some numbers to drive the point home. If you borrowed $15,900 toward a car at 4.9% for five years, you would pay $299/month. If you kept the car and made all the payments and paid it off by the due date, you would have paid $1,260 in interest. What would happen if you had a three year loan on that same car instead of a five year? The payment would be $475/month, but in three years you would own the car outright. You would have also only paid $757 in interest and you wouldn't have risked being upside down on the loan.

Now let's compare two people who bought a $20,000 car and both had the same $16,700 loan. Say the first person took out a 3 year loan, and the second person took a five. Let's assume further that after 3 years, the car is worth $6,000 (a reasonable estimate). After 3 years the first person has an asset worth $6,000 that they owe nothing on. The second person, at 36 months still owes $7,000 so they have an asset that is worth less then they owe...in other words they have a liability of $1,000.

"But I can't afford $475/month for a car payment" you might say. Well, then you can't afford a $20,000 car, or you need more of a down payment. Don't make the mistake of buying the car that you like if you can't afford it. The dealership is not on your side, they want to make a sale, and they don't care if it ends up costing you in the long run. Who can blame them, they are in the business of selling cars, not providing financial advice, right?

I suggest you not take a loan more than three years, but if you have to push it, then you might go four years. If you do go four years, try to make extra payments to pay it off early. This will save you on interest and also end the risk of being upside down.

Once you finish paying off your car, consider still making the monthly payment to your savings, as if you still owe on the car. In another two years, you will probably have enough money to buy your next car for cash! Let's consider the first guy in my example above. After three years, if he continues to put away $475/month for the next 2 years he will have saved $11,400, not considering interest or gain on the investment. That is a nice amount of money to be able to put away.

You might argue that the person who was paying $299 has an extra $176/month ($475 vs. $299 payment) and I agree, but is that second person really saving the $176 each month? Probably not, because they got the five year loan because they couldn't afford to pay the car off in a shorter period of time, which means they really couldn't afford the car they bought.

Buy vs. Lease

Several people have asked me whether it's better to buy a car or lease one. To me this question is like asking whether it's better to own a house or rent.

Let's use the $20,000 car again for this explanation. If you buy a car, then after you finish making payments the title is turned over to you and you own the car. The timing of getting another car, after the loan is paid is really up to you. You are left with a car and can do with it what you please. At that point, you can either keep the car and drive it until it doesn't run anymore, or you could trade it in or sell it on your own at some point and use that money for another car, or for something else.

If you lease a car, then you are making payments for the use of someone else's car, just like you would when you rent an apartment. When you are done, you turn over the keys to the other person and you have to get a new car. At this point, you no longer have a car, so you will most likely need to enter into another lease transaction right away, or buy a car.

You might say that when you lease, that the monthly payment is less. Likely that is true, just like the monthly rent payment is usually less than a mortgage payment. Technically you are "buying" the portion of the life of the vehicle that you are using, but not the rest. To say that a different way, the car dealer selling you the $20,000 car would assume that at the end of a 3 year lease the car would be worth $9,800, so in that case you would basically be paying them $10,200 plus interest. The dealerships have a reasonable idea what the car will be worth, and when you trade it back in, they will compare what they thought it would be worth, to the condition you turn it in and then tell you if you are even or if you owe them more because the condition is less than ideal. Sometimes people find that they have to pay the dealer another $500, or even more.   Read the terms before signing the lease.

Which one is better?   Well, if you are a person who likes a new car every 3 years, then you might want to lease, assuming you get a good rate and good deal compared to buying. On the other hand, if you want to keep a car for some time, or your financial condition is such that you should be keeping the car for the long run, then buying will be the best option.

Personally, I think there is more guess work in leasing and so I think that should be left to businesses rather than individuals.

Upside down loans

What happens if you already have a car that you took out a five year loan on and now it is upside down? Start making additional payments each month. Also, consider gap insurance. Gap insurance provides car insurance for the difference between the value of the car and the amount you owe. So if you were to total your car and you owed $10,000 but the book value is only $7,000, you regular car insurance will only pay you out $7,000. They don't care that you owe an additional $3,000 on the car. That is your problem, not theirs.

The gap insurance policy will pay the $3,000 if you were to be in that situation, however. You should weigh the cost of the gap insurance premium as compared to the value the policy will provide. If you are paying $100/month on the policy and you are only upside down by say $500, then after month 6 you will have paid more in gap insurance premiums than you would have had to pay if the car was totaled. Gap insurance is only if you are in a bad position and there is no other way to cover yourself for that risk. See Chapter 6 about insurance and what I say about the cost vs. value of insurance. Only get what you need and don't pay for what you will never use.

In no way am I advocating for Gap insurance, it isn't a solution when you go into buying a car, instead you should buy with a shorter term, and this is just a bandage for the wound if you are already upside down.

I have also seen people who were upside down on a car trade that car in for another one.   Somehow they believe this will help the situation, but it really doesn't. If you owe more than a car is worth, the dealership will take a trade in on a new/newer car and offer to roll over the extra amount you owe to the new car. What did you really just do? Essentially you bought another car for more than it's worth.

You are still upside down, just now on a more expensive car.   Don't do that to yourself.

Generally speaking it's best to keep the current car you have until you can pay it off, then consider another car, but be sure to get one you can afford this time, or keep the one you have and start putting away the monthly payment for when you really _need_, not just _want_ a new car.

New vs. Used

The next question regarding cars is whether to buy a new car or not. This is also a personal decision, where you can make the argument for either side.

The new car argument is that you know that no one abused the car before you and you have the full history. Also because the car is new, it should last you longer than a used car.

On the opposite side of the argument, the engine quality (and to a great extent the oil quality) in cars these days means that the engine should last you

100,000 miles or even a lot more. With that said if you can buy a car new for $20,000 and you can get a 2 year old version with 30,000 mile on it for $12,000 you saved $8,000 and got almost the same amount of useful life from the car. It's definitely worth the consideration.

Back in 2008, I bought a used 2004 Audi A4 with 75,000 miles on it for $12,800. Yes, this was more of a luxury car, but new it was probably about $45,000. I saved over $30,000 on this car compared to new. As a single guy at the time (dating my wife) and with all the other areas of my financial life in order, I thought why not?   In 2011 when I sold the car, I had about 140,000 miles on it and sold it for $7,500. That means I drove a luxury sport car for 3 years and it only cost me $5,300. The guy who bought it brand new lost well over $30,000 in 4 years and I only lost $5,300.   Who got more value? You be the judge.

When I sold the car, it was at a point in its life when it was starting to need considerable replacement parts, so it could have started to be a bit of a money pit, but when I bought a new car, the cost of that new car was much more than the car I had.   If I put $3,000 or even $5,000 into the Audi, it would have run like a champ for a long period of time. It might have been worth doing, but I decided to sell it.

 I sold it because after getting married and planning for a family, I wanted something a bit more practical. I'll keep my current car (Mitsubishi Outlander) for at least 6 years or more, so I will get good value from it, but there is no question that it was more out of pocket expense than keeping the Audi would be.

Car buying summary

I started off this chapter stating that the cheapest car you will ever own is the one you already have, so if you are trying to get ahead and implement the other strategies I detail in this book, then keep your current car as long as you can.

A car loses value the minute you drive it off the lot. It's no longer a new car, but a used one. Look up the value of a used model year car vs. new. You'll see the difference.

According to Edmunds.com the average car loses 11% as soon as you drive it off the lot. Within the first five years of ownership the car depreciates by 15-25% each year and is worth around 40% of what you paid after 5 years. The more expensive the car is, the more you lose.

The longer you keep your current car, the newer the next one will be. How is that possible? Well, if you only buy new cars and you have 2011 model and keep it for only 3 years, then your next car will be a 2014. The person who keeps their car for 5 years gets a 2016 next. Before long the person who keeps their car for 2 years longer will have bought one less car than the other person, which means a big savings. Remember, a car is a depreciable asset. You buy it and the value keeps going down. At a certain point, the depreciation gets much smaller, so the longer you keep a car, the more value you get and the less money you lose.

CHAPTER 5

BUYING A HOUSE

Is a house purchase next on your list?

Fast forward a few years and now you are starting to make more money in your career and you have begun to see your financial resources grow nicely. How about buying a house?

If you already own a home, don't skip this section. Read the part about refinancing as well.

The decision to buy or continue to rent requires some consideration. Clearly, the American Dream includes home ownership, but a home should be considered a place to live, not an asset that will make you rich when you sell it a few years later. Further, if you don't believe you will live in a particular area for more than 3-5 years, you might want to keep renting so you aren't stuck when you want to relocate. On the other hand, if you can afford to buy a house and you believe that in the next few years home prices will go up, it's better to buy sooner to get into the housing market at the current prices than wait until later.

One final consideration (though there could be dozens more) would be to compare the rental rate you would pay, to a mortgage payment. you could pay much less in rent than you would pay on a mortgage and you can invest the rest of the money in a wise growth investment, then it might make sense to continue to rent.

If you think you may be ready to buy, and you have your down payment ready, have calculated how much you can afford, and have a feel for what size mortgage you can qualify for a pay for , you may be well on your way. There are plenty of articles on determining how much house you can afford. Consider discussing with your bank, but keep in mind that the general rule is not to spend more than 30%

of your income on housing. Also, remember that a mortgage broker will make a commission based on the amount you borrow, so if they tell you that you can get a mortgage for $300,000 and you think you can only afford $250,000 then go with the more conservative number to avoid the pitfalls that many have made in the past decade or so. Remember, just because someone says you can afford a certain amount of borrowing – which makes them more commission – doesn't mean you should borrow that much. A general rule is not to spend more than 30% of your income on housing.

In the late 1990's through 2007, the cost of borrowing was so low and financing options were many. As a result, people tended to take out loans that did not suit their best interest and also purchased homes that were out of their reach conventionally. This phenomenon drove up the cost of homes, but like any bubble, it can only grow so large before it bursts. Some people even took the money out of their home equity by refinancing with cash out and spent it on vacations, cars and other personal items. That didn't play out too well for most of them.

If someone told you that you can buy a $100,000 sports car for only $550 a month would you do it? Ok, what is your answer to that question? Was your answer "Yes, where do I sign up?" If so, you answered incorrectly. You should have asked a question and that is: For how many years and what is the interest rate? What if that loan was for 20 years? The car would be long gone before you could pay it off. Buying a house is one of the biggest financial investments a person makes. Make sure you ask the right questions and know what you are getting. If you aren't sure, it's cheaper to pay a lawyer a few hundred dollars to explain it to you than to lose a house and damage your credit.

Let's go back to the $100,000 sports car analogy. What if I tell you that you pay $300 a month for the car for the first 2 years and then after that you still owe the full $100,000 on the car? Now you have to pay that $100,000 off over the next 2 years at the rate of $58,000 per year? Are you still interested in the car? The average person is going to say "There is no way I can afford that."

This is exactly what happened with the housing market.   People took out loans without knowing exactly what they were getting themselves into. Also, because the money appeared to be so cheap, rather than sticking with the rule that you shouldn't buy a home more than 3-5 times your salary, or the one that says your mortgage shouldn't be more than roughly 30% of your monthly expenses, people were borrowing upwards of 5 times their salary and 50% or more of their monthly salary. If they lost their job for a short period of time, and they didn't have a rainy day fund to help pay that mortgage while they were out of work and they couldn't take a lower paying job, because it wouldn't cover their mortgage plus other expenses. Many ended up losing their homes.

Give yourself cushion and do not buy all the house you are told you can afford. Buy something simpler or a bit less expensive and then when you have significant equity, consider upgrading your home.

Always remember that your monthly payment for your house will typically include the principal (amount you still owe) and interest on the loan, plus most mortgages will also incorporate the property taxes and insurance into your monthly payment, so when you are thinking about the principal and interest and if you can afford that payment, layer in the annual property taxes and insurance cost (divided into 12 monthly payments), to get a better picture of what your payment will be. Remember that if your taxes or cost of insurance goes up the next year, so will your monthly payments. Make sure you can really afford it.

Upgrades to your home?

Now that you own your home, should you start making updates and upgrades to it? The simple answer is maybe.

The first thing you want to consider is whether the upgrade will make the house more valuable, or whether it is something that will make the place more comfortable for you if you are going to live there for a long time. Keep in mind that if you make costly changes to the home that are outside of what a typical home in the area would consist of, you may be making your home less marketable. In other words, if you convert the garage into another room, someone looking for a home with a garage may not want to buy your house. If you change the kitchen into a recreation room, again the market value for a home with no kitchen is not very good. You can ask area realtors what upgrades tend to result in adding to the value and what ones don't.

If money is tight and you can live without making that major renovation, then save up until you can afford it. Stick with the simple inexpensive changes until you can afford to do more. If you are handy, consider doing some work yourself, to save on the contractor costs. Just remember, if you don't know what you are doing, the damage you can cause to the home can outweigh any savings from doing it yourself.

Always remember though, that if an average house in your town or neighborhood sells for around $200,000, you aren't going to get $300,000 because you made $100,000 worth of renovations to the home. Someone who wants a $300,000 house will buy in a different neighborhood.

Make Extra Mortgage Payments?

When people buy their home, they start making mortgage payments month after month without giving it any extra thought. Ever consider making extra payments to lower the principal amount? You can apply part of a bonus, a tax refund check or even add an extra $100 or so per month toward your mortgage and pay down your balance faster. If you were to pay $100 extra per month on a $200,000 mortgage at 5% interest, you would save almost $37,000 over the course of the loan. Think about making extra payments as putting away money in a bank account earning 5% on your "deposit"(if your loan is at 5%).

Typically people choose a 30 year mortgage, but it could be worth looking at a 20 year or even 15 year loan, which could save you money in the long run. A shorter term can help you own your house outright much quicker as well. Because the loan period is shorter, the interest rates are usually lower. For example, as of the date of this writing a well-qualified buyer can get a 30 year mortgage at 3.72%, whereas a 15 year loan is at 2.92% according to Bankrate.com. Keep in mind, these are historically low rates, so as rates go up, there could be a bigger difference between the two. Using the same $200,000 loan amount you would pay $132,218 in interest over 30 years with a monthly principal and interest payment of $923 per month. The same amount borrowed at 15 years would cost you $1,374 per month, ($451 more per month), but you would only pay $47,227 in interest. That is a savings of $84,991 over the course of the loan, not to mention the fact that year 16 you would have an additional $923 a month in your pocket. We are talking some serious savings just for a little bit of pain up front. Give it some thought.

Should I refinance?

You may have read about the historically low rates I mentioned and then realize that you are paying 5%, 6% or even more on your current mortgage. Should you refinance that mortgage to a lower rate? The answer depends on how long you are going to stay in your home. If you have no intentions of moving then anything more than a half to 1% reduction is typically going to save you money.

I'll give you a tool that you can use to help you with the calculations. If you have Microsoft Excel, open it and click on "File" select "New", and one of the templates available is called "Loan amortization schedule". You just type in the mortgage amount, interest rate, number of years, payments per year and the date the loan starts and it will calculate the payments (principal and interest). You can then change the interest rate to the lower rate and see what your savings would be. For example, if your current mortgage balance is $200,000 and your current rate is 5%, and you have 15 years left to pay on your mortgage, by refinancing to 3.5% you would save $151 per month or about $27,000 over the remaining loan period.

Keep in mind that the bank will charge you a fee to close on the new loan. Consider the fees they charge, which can be anywhere from $1,000 to $3,000 or more. Clearly if you were to keep this loan for the full 15 years, you are paying that fee but the savings more than make up for it. Where it could actually cost you more is if you were to move soon after refinancing. You need to add up the monthly savings; multiplied by the number of months it will take for that savings to equal the fees you paid. If you are going to be in your house long enough to recover that cost, then it's worth refinancing.

One pitfall to remember is that if you only have 15 years left on your current mortgage (or any amount of time less than 30 years), do you really want to refinance back to a new 30 year mortgage?

Don't let a dishonest mortgage broker tell you that your payments will be much lower by refinancing, when they are putting you back into a 30 year mortgage. It is true that the payments will be lower, but because the loan period is longer, you may actually pay more interest. (See my point above about paying your mortgage in a shorter time period and saving money). Don't let someone compare apples to oranges and tell you that you will be saving more money, when you are only extending the number of years of your loan. You will save money monthly, but the number of payments will be more, so you will end up paying more in total.

Having said that, if you are in a situation where you can't afford your monthly payment, because you had to take a lower paying job or other expenses are squeezing you, then refinancing to a longer term would be much better than damaging your credit score due to missed payments, or risking losing the house.

Buying a house is a major investment. Be sure you have the right information and that your financial situation is sufficient to make such an investment.

Be sure you research the housing market and that you are confident you are paying the right price and you are financing the house in an advantageous way before you embark on the journey. If you aren't sure, definitely get the information you need and don't go blindly into buying a house just because you like one. It can be a financial disaster for you if you don't do it right and a great value if you do it properly.

CHAPTER 6

INSURANCE

Now that you have accumulated a considerable amount of wealth, and you have put check marks next to all of the above considerations, you probably have some amount of debt and maybe you have a family to support.

These are all great things and also, a reason to make sure you have the proper insurance to go along with your rainy day fund.

What would happen if you were permanently disabled, or worse, if you died? Would your family be able to sustain their standard of living without having your income to rely on? Consider disability and life insurance.

Do you have the right amount of medical coverage, so that if you were hospitalized for a considerable amount of time, or your loved one is, you can get them the best medical care and you don't break the bank and end up on the street?

If you are aging and you don't want your children to have to pay for a nursing home if you were to need one, you should consider long term care insurance.

Insurance is an important safeguard to be certain that your loved ones are taken care of if you can't take care of them. Insurance is not an area where I will offer recommendations other than to suggest you consult several agents to get what is right for your family. Just like with buying a house, make sure you understand what you are getting with an insurance policy. If you don't understand it, ask lots of questions. Don't assume that because the agent offers you the policy, then it's got to be one that fits your needs.

This chapter is quite short, but that should not diminish how important it is to preserve what you have worked hard to accumulate.

Remember, insurance is the biggest waste of money....until you need it. What happens if you don't have it when you need it? Doesn't that cost way more than the premiums?

You can typically get insurance for any type of situation, so make sure you have the protection you need. Don't just know that you have a car insurance policy or homeowners, but know if that policy covers passengers in your car or contractors in your home. Don't guess and hop your coverage is adequate, understand your needs and be sure you are covered.

CHAPTER 7

INVESTMENT STRATEGIES

Now that you have tackled the essential savings and put aside a rainy day fund, you have bought a house, or maybe you are just putting the money aside to buy a house, the question is, what do I do with my cash?

One alternative is to put it in a bank account, which is FDIC insured, so it is safe and you know your money will be there. The question is will inflation take up more of your money than you earn in interest payments on your "safe" bank account? For the last few years, savings accounts offer returns of less than 1%. In many cases it is much less than 1%, so you could actually be losing money by putting it in the bank. How is that possible? As my college professor Mr. Klein would say, "Inflation is the silent killer". Let's look at an example of how.

For the purpose of this example, let's assume that the bank will give you 2% and you decide to put $1 in the bank. Let's further assume that if you didn't put that $1 in the bank, you would have spent it on a pen, which costs $1 today. After a year goes by, you look in your bank account and now your $1 has grown to be worth $1.02. That's great news, right? Now you can take your $1.02 and go buy that pen you wanted, but unfortunately you learn that pens now cost $1.05. Even though you thought you made 2 cents, you actually lost 3 cents worth of buying power. Think of the cost of the pen as being a benchmark for the cost of everything in the economy. So whether it's the pen or anything else you are buying, the point is you lost buying power, because everything is now more expensive than it was the year before. Now you can't afford as much. That is what happens in a period of inflation.

How do you combat the inflation problem? Well, you have to make at least 5% in that example just to have the exact same buying power a year later, so if you want your money to grow, you should be earning 6% or even higher. Keep in mind that the percentages I am using here are just for example purposes, so there could be times you need a higher return, or even times when 2% or 3% is plenty to stay ahead of inflation. It just depends on the economy. So you ask, what are alternatives to putting your money into the bank? Generally speaking those options are stocks and bonds. Yes, there are many other forms of investment, to include real estate, precious metals, art etc., but for purposes of this book we are keeping it to things the average person can use.

Stocks

Most people understand that stock is an investment in a company, but generally speaking it is also ownership in that company, if it is regular common stock.   Each share of stock is a vote related to management decisions in a business. With that said, if a company has 100 million shares and you own 1 share, your vote isn't going to do much to sway the direction of the company.

Why do companies issue stock? It is because they believe they can get the highest amount of money to run the business or for the creators of the business to cash out. Take Facebook as an example, the owners invested a lot of time and money in creating the company. They probably borrowed money from a bank to help fund the day to day operations and might have enough revenue from advertising to show a profit. At a certain point, the owners decided they could get a nice payout for their investment by selling shares of their ownership to other people, so they make that available to the public in an Initial Public Offering (IPO). People then decided that they believed each share was worth a certain price, based on the suggested price that the broker set when crunching the numbers for what they believed the value was and what people would be willing to pay to own the stock.

That might be more than you wanted to know, but basically after an IPO, then the market dictates where the stock price goes. Obviously if a company makes more money, then the stock value should go up. If things aren't looking so good, it should go down.   There are other times when investors are just putting money into the market or taking it out based on their thoughts about the economy and a stock can benefit or be hurt by that action even if it had nothing to do with the value of that particular stock.

So how do you know when to buy a stock? The easy answer is when a stock is a good value. The hard part is determining the value in a stock.

It is hard to determine the value, because no one has a crystal ball that will tell them if the market is going to rise or go down. Once the market moves in one direction or another, you already missed the increase or got crushed by the down side.

The average person will look at a stock that is going up and buy it because the price has risen, but does that mean you are buying a stock that is priced too high? It could be. Other people go off a tip from a friend or family member who says they own the stock. Are you sure they are giving you good advice? Are they sure?

The way to look at the value of a stock is return on investment. If the company is losing money and they will continue to lose money for a long time, it may not be a good place to put your money, unless they think they may be on to something that will turn a profit, but it's likely to be highly risky.

If a company is making money, however it's worth a look to see if the stock is something you want to own. I would first ask myself if it is a product or service that is sustainable and perhaps even something you would use yourself, or at least could see the majority of people wanting to use. Let's use Johnson & Johnson (J&J) as an example. They have been around for a long time and they continually make a nice profit. So you might be interested in buying their stock. It's price has gone up significantly this year and so you think you will buy. Is it a good deal? In the interest of full disclosure, I worked for J&J in the past, though I do not currently own any of their stock directly, though it is perhaps a component in my retirement account.   I am not using them as an example in such a way as to recommend or not recommend buying their stock, but rather just sharing based on a company I am somewhat familiar with. The following measures can be good ways to determine the value of a stock.

Price/Earnings Ratio (PE)

To the average person that term means nothing, but it is a great measure of a company. Simply put, it is taking the stock price divided by the earnings. So with J&J trading at about $89 a share and its annual earnings being $4.62 per share, you get a price/earnings ratio of about 19 times earnings. Said differently, that means it would take about 19 years before the earnings of the company – assuming earnings stay the same – would return the full amount you invested if you bought a share at $89 today. By comparison, Pfizer – a J&J competitor- is selling for $29 a share with earnings per share at $3.02, so their price/earnings ratio is 9.55, meaning you would recover your investment just in earnings in less than 10 years.

The price/earnings ratio isn't enough to decide one stock is better than the other, but it is a way to gauge the two companies.

Dividend payout

Another measure of stocks is how much of a dividend they pay out. If you get cash today that is also a return on your investment. By comparison J&J offers a dividend yield of 66 cents per share each quarter while Pfizer pays out 24 cents per share. You might say that the J&J dividend is much better because it pays a much bigger dividend, but if you compare 66 cents (times 4 quarters per year) to the $89 cost per share that is 2.97%, whereas the 24 cents on Pfizer is 3.33%

This would still only be a part of the equation, because you are only comparing two companies and you would also want to know which one is more likely to continue its profitability, which company is larger and a host of other factors, but as you research the stocks you will get a better feel for the various comparisons.

Compare Apples to Apples

You will notice that I compared J&J to Pfizer and not to Wal-Mart, or Verizon for example. You need to be sure you are comparing companies within the same industry, because a PE Ratio in one industry might be very different from that of another. For example, Google is selling at a PE of 27 and Apple at 11.5.

That being said, if a company is selling at a PE of greater that its industry leaders, it may not be the best place to put your money. Then again, if they are the market leader and you see the value they have over their competitors, that higher PE might make sense.

Bonds

Think of bonds as the opposite of stock. Whereas stock is equity, meaning you are buying ownership in someone's company, bonds are where you are buying someone's debt. A different way to say this is that you are lending money to the company that you buy the bond from and you are entitled to be paid back at the rate set on the bond. Companies and government entities (Federal, states and municipalities) will issue bonds rather than going to the bank to borrow money. This is usually because they can get a better deal by issuing the bonds than they can get by borrowing from a bank, or because the amount they are borrowing is more than any one bank might be willing or able to lend.

So if you buy a $100 Federal Savings Bond, then you basically lent the government $100 which they promise to pay back in a set period of time with interest.

There are two common ways the borrower handles the interest portion:

1. They pay you interest on a regular basis, by sending you a check monthly, quarterly or annually
    OR
2.   They can issue the bond for lower than the amount that gets paid out in the end.

The first one is pretty self-explanatory, they just pay you interest each period and then you get your $100 investment back at the end. The second, which is how Federal bonds are usually issued, is that they will sell a $100 bond for say $80 and then when it matures then you get $100. In the latter case, you don't get any interest paid to you during the period you hold the bond, you just get a bigger amount than you paid at the end and that extra $20 is essentially the interest.

The best way to explain this is that the interest rate is built into what they are selling the bond for. So in the case of the regular interest bearing bond, if it yields 2%, then each year you are getting $2 in interest payments and then if it is a 10 year bond, at the end of 10 years they give you $100 back when you cash in the bond at it's due date (known as maturity date). On the second type of bond, you don't get any interest; you basically get a lower price when you buy it. For example you pay $80 for the bond and in year 10 you get $100.   If you did the calculation that would mean a little less than 2%, but you get the idea.

It sounds like bonds are a pretty secure investment right? That is true if you consider the fact that you know exactly what you paid and how much you will get when the bond matures, but there is a risk involved. To be clear, there are two risks, one is the risk of default – meaning the bond issuer goes bankrupt and can't pay you, the other is interest rate risk.

What is interest rate risk, you ask? What happens if you buy a bond for $100 that pays 2% and then next year because rates go up, a bond you can buy then will pay you a 3% return? No one would want to keep a bond that pays 2% when they can buy one that pays 3%, so now – just like with inflation- if you keep the 2% bond, you are losing out on the opportunity to make $1 extra per year times 10 years.

The problem you find then is that if you try to sell your bond that earns 2% to someone else, they don't want it; because they know they can buy a 3% bond. The only way you can sell your 2% bond is if you are willing to sell it for less than the $100 you paid for it. That is a normal part of the bond market.

Let's look at it the other way, and assume you had a 4% bond and the going rate was 3%, someone might be willing to pay you more than $100 to buy your bond, because it pays out a higher rate.

That is the basic way bonds work. If you keep it for the whole time you get your full money back, but think back to my pencil example, if you get $105 and you need $110 to buy what $100 bought a few years back, then you lost money.

Stocks vs. Bonds

Generally speaking, stocks and bonds will work in inverse to each other. This is partly because a dollar can only be invested in stocks or bonds, (not considering other investments) so if you take your money out of one, you would put it in the other. I understand that there are dozens of other investments if not more, but stocks and bonds are the most common for the average investor. Generally speaking you should own both and mutual funds will have both in a particular percentage mix of assets.

If you own a bond, you hold the debt of a company and if they were to go bankrupt, you get paid before a stockholder does, so your money is more secure in that sense.

Also, bonds offer a guaranteed rate of return whereas the stocks could go down in a bad stock market. Assuming the company is one that will be successful in the future; the bond secures your value at a certain number, whereas the stock doesn't guarantee any return. On the other hand, the value of the stock could go way up and the bond would just stay at the same rate of return.

Just like most things in life, there are advantages and disadvantages to stocks and bonds. Most people will have some level of investment in each.

Mutual Funds

Most of us have mutual funds either in a retirement account or ones we bought ourselves. However, typically people don't know exactly what a mutual fund is.

Remember the children's story of Rock Soup? It goes like this: There was one villager who noticed that people in the village didn't have enough food for a meal, so he devised a "trick" of sorts, where he told people he was making rock soup, which was nothing more than water and a rock in a big pot. One villager offered to contribute potatoes if he could have some rock soup, another offered carrots and so on. In the end, everyone had a hearty meal because they all pooled their resources into one big pot.

A mutual fund is very similar. Let's assume you have $1,000 to invest. Perhaps you could buy 20 shares of a $50 stock. Now all your money is in one stock. Another person could take their $1,000 and buy $1,000 worth of bonds, while yet another buys

$1,000 worth of silver. Each person has exposure to their investment's ups and downs and nothing else. If they are willing to pool all their resources together, now they have "rock soup" known as a mutual fund.

Instead of each person owning $1,000 worth of one particular investment, now each of the investors own 1/3 of a diversified portfolio of 20 stocks 1 bond worth $1,000 and silver worth $1,000.   Multiply that by many more people and many more investments and you have what is hopefully a balanced mutual fund with the risk well distributed amongst various asset classes. Asset classes are simply the group or type of asset, such as bonds, stocks, precious metals etc.

One thing you want to be sure of is that when you invest in multiple mutual funds that they all have different things they invest in.   What if you had 3 mutual funds and each invested heavily in the top 10 largest US companies. If those 10 companies did poorly, all three of your funds would do poorly. If, instead one mutual fund invested in the 10 largest companies and one invested in gold and silver and yet another invested in bonds, there is a good chance that not all 3 would go down at the same time and one would go up when another was going down.   That is diversification. Don't simply put your money in several funds because they all have different names and assume you are diversified. Each mutual fund has a prospectus which tells you about how it has done in the past and what it invests in. Be sure that it is doing well and that it doesn't duplicate what you have in another investment.

CHAPTER 8

<u>INVESTMENT TECHNIQUES</u>

Dollar Cost Averaging

"Buy low, sell high." That's the conventional wisdom with respect to making a profit on anything. The question is how do you know when something is high and when it's low?

There have been studies where they take monkeys and give them a page of the Wall Street Journal and they buy the investment the monkey points to. They then compare that to what sophisticated investors choose and you will find times that the monkey chooses better. While that is typically luck, so is picking the winner every time in the market, even if you are a professional. If professional investors and advisors could make money every time, they wouldn't be offering their services to you, but rather buying everything they can for themselves.

Don't misunderstand the above comments. There is considerable value in professional advisors, because they know how to crunch the numbers and they have read up on what is good and bad, but the point is that they can't guarantee any type of return. If they tell you they can, then run, because they may be related to Bernie Madoff.

Many people attempt to time the market by buying at one point and then hoping to sell when the investment goes up. The problem is no one knows when it will go up, or if it might go down. That is where dollar cost averaging comes in.

It is really a simple concept that can make investing disciplined for you.

For illustration purposes, I will talk about one investment, but you should diversify.

Let's say, for example you decide to invest $100 per month and that investment XYZ appeals to you. Today XYZ sells for $1 a share. Maybe you think it could go down or could go up. Do you wait around to find out? I suggest you don't.

So, invest your $100 into XYZ and you get 100 shares. When next month comes around, XYZ is selling for $1.05 per share, this time you only get 95 shares, but the first 100 shares you bought made 5 cents each in profit. In the third month, the value goes down to $1.03 per share, so you invest your same $100 and get 97 shares. Now, your second month shares lost 2 cents each, but you are still up from the first month.

Doing the math, you now have 292 shares for the price of $300. At $1.03 per share your investment is worth $300.76.

As you can see you still made money. Keep doing this every month for the year.

What if you waited until month 3, thinking the price would go down and just saved the cash in your checking account? You would have had your $300 that you put aside in cash and investing all at once, you could only buy 291 shares, instead of the 292 you now have.

These are small numbers, but the example can hold true to yield considerable gains.

Truly, no investment is without risk, but when you find a good one, and invest in a disciplined manner, your money has a good chance to grow.

When the price is down, think of it as buying the investment when it is "on sale". You get more shares for your dollar. Who doesn't like a sale?

This strategy allows you to be disciplined in your investing, assuming you believe in the value of the investment in which you are putting your money.

Clearly while doing this, you should be monitoring your investments to make sure they are still sound.

I don't mean micromanaging them and selling because the market went down a bit, but rather making sure the value is still there. For example, just because the stock price of J&J went down by $1 doesn't mean you should sell, but if you invested in Blackberry and they are saying they don't think they will make it, then it might be time to consider a new investment before the stock tanks.

Dogs of the Dow

A few years ago, when reading some financial websites, I came across the term "Dogs of the Dow". At first I didn't know exactly what that meant, but the recommendation was that some of them would be a good investment.

I learned that the term meant Dow Jones listed stocks that had a price that was low compared to the dividend it pays out. When the stock market is not moving dramatically up or down, if you hold a non-dividend paying stock, which was $25 on January 1st it might be worth $24.50 now, or maybe it's worth $25.10. Either way, not much happened for your return on investment.

If you have a dividend paying stock, however, then even if the stock was still at exactly $25 a share, you earned a dividend payout, so you have more cash in hand. That might not be a bad idea, right?

If you are talking about a small company stock, there might be risk in owning that stock, but if you own a stock that is part of the Dow Jones Industrial Average, probably it's a fairly solid company. Clearly, there could be risk on either stock, but you have less risk in a big, well established company.

So to understand what makes it a "dog" you look at the price of the stock when you bought it (or today if you don't own it yet) and compare it to the dividend that is being paid out. If that dividend is a nice percentage compared to many others, it's worth a look.

Let's take Verizon for example. In 2012 it was trading at around $40 a share and it paid a dividend quarterly that equals $1.95 per share per year. So $1.95 divided by $40 = 4.875%. Even if the stock price goes up, you bought in at $40, so your rate of return on the dividend stays the same. If you buy when the stock goes up, the dividend rate drops and vice-versa.

 Just use the simple formula: Dividend/Stock Price to get your dividend yield, or check out a website that provides stock data to get that information.

That means if you put your money in Verizon at the beginning of the year, at the end of the year you have earned around 4.8% on your investment. Considering that banks are giving less than 1/2% on deposits, this is a really good return.

Of course you do run the risk that the stock price could drop, but you get that risk with any stock.

There are good reasons to own stocks and no investment strategy is perfect for everyone, but it might be worth a look at the Dogs of the Dow as a part of your investment strategy.

Rebalancing

If you invest in mutual funds or even individual stocks, you should consider how you want to balance your asset mix. If you want 50% stocks, 30% bonds and 20% in commodities such as precious metals, you should make sure that balance remains in your account. Keep in mind I am not making an argument that this is a proper mix, nor that any one mix is the right formula for everyone, but if that was your assessment you want to make sure you maintain that.

Let's say you had $100,000 invested on January 1 of year 1 and you therefore had $50,000 in stocks, $30,000 in bonds and $20,000 in commodities based on the above desired mix. When January 1 year 2 rolls around, you might find that stocks did well, so now 52% of your money value is in stocks, let's say that 27% is now in bonds, because they didn't do as well and 21% is in commodities based on the results of year 1. So maybe now you have $110,000. If you want to maintain the same 50/30/20 mix, you would need to sell 2% of your stock portfolio and 1% of the commodities and invest that into bonds. This is rebalancing. The idea is that next year, the result could be different and one of the other investment types would go up.

Another situation where you might use rebalancing is with your mutual funds. You might put 25% into each of Fund A, B, C and D in your 401(k) when you start your job. Next year you look and see the balance is 20% in each of fund A, B and C and 40% in Fund D. If you believe in what each fund holds, then you would sell some of D and allocate that into each of Funds A-C to get you back in balance of 25% per fund. What you will find is that the following year, Fund D might be down a bit and the other funds are up. Perhaps all of them are up, but Fund D is up by less than the percentage the other ones are up. If you didn't rebalance and after a few years you have a large amount in one of the funds, you have your proverbial eggs heavily weighted into one basket.

Generally speaking, you will do well to keep rebalancing so that your risk continues to be spread out over each fund. If not, you could end up with 50% (or more) in one fund and if that fund does poorly, half your portfolio could take a major hit. If you have 25% in each of 4 quality funds, then only 25% of your money will take a major hit of one fund goes down.   Perhaps you consider 10% in each of 10 funds or some combination that fits your goals. Either way, you don't want to heavily weight your investment into one fund or into one place. Diversification is generally the key to financial safety.

Dividend Reinvestment Plans (DRIP)

May stocks, as well as portfolios will offer what is called a dividend reinvestment plan or sometimes it is referred to by its acronym DRIP. What this means is that if you own a stock, you can take the dividends and have them buy more shares of the same stock or investment with those funds.

Going back to my Verizon example, let's assume you own 100 shares of Verizon and it pays out 53 cents per share as a dividend, then each quarter you get $53. You can ask the portfolio to take that $53 and buy more Verizon shares. Sometimes you can only buy whole shares, so that if Verizon was selling at $43, you could only buy 1 share and keep the $10. Other times they will let you buy fractional shares, so that you would get 1.2 shares with your $53. Either way, you get more shares, which means larger future dividends.

Assuming the same investment, then in the next quarter you have 101 shares and get paid $53.53 in dividend income. The following quarter, you have 102 shares and get paid $54.06. As time goes by, you dramatically increase your share ownership and your dividend income.

This is just scratching the surface of the types of investment strategies there are out there. Keep in mind that you should start with a sound strategy and don't let emotion cloud your vision. Do the smart thing and continue to read on other strategies.

Once you become a more sophisticated investor and you see things going well, learn about new strategies, but remember not to go for the Hail Mary pass. That is a losing strategy. Create a sound and disciplined investment plan and stick with it over the long haul. There will be times to take risk and there will be times to review the plan, but be sure to have your strategy, rather than hope for the best based on emotions or random tips. Invest consistently and wisely and watch your funds grow.

CONCLUSION

When I was a teenager my mother told me "Money once spoke and it said 'He who minds me, I'll mind". I hope that what I have shared here has provided you with helpful insights on personal finance in an easy to understand methodology and in an order that makes sense. This is by no means everything you can learn, nor everything I can teach, but it is a great start.

Keep in mind, that regardless of how you save, the time is now. The sooner you start saving the more likely you will be to secure a successful future for yourself and your family.

In the end, it is about leaving a legacy. Will you leave others with positive values from which they can grow and share, or will you waste golden opportunities?

Remember, with anything you learn, it is lost if not shared, so learn all you can and share it with others.

If you take anything away from this book - and I hope you take a lot – know this: People aren't rich because they make a lot of money. No, they are rich because they keep the money they make. Now it definitely doesn't hurt to make a lot, but plenty of athletes, actors and even the average lottery winner end up bankrupt in a few years. Why? Because they spend what they make, and often, much more than they make.

 On the opposite side, people like my parents raised a family of 4 children with one income, as my mother stayed home with us. My dad was a blue collar worker and didn't make a fortune either. The key was that both my parents understood the value of doing without unnecessary material things. The result is that at age 55, my father was able to retire with a comfortable savings. How did they do it?

They implemented many of the strategies noted in this book.

For example, they bought houses that needed some work and saved a lot by fixing up the houses themselves. They have owned only 6 cars in the last 40 years and they ate most meals at home.

Don't assume this meant they were missing out on living. They took a family vacation every single summer and built great memories with their children. They owned a vacation place in a campground where we spent our summers as we were growing up. We went to fairs, carnivals, amusement parks, you name it. Of course, we didn't have every new toy or a new bicycle every few years. We learned to hold onto and take care of the things we had.

The key question you need to ask yourself is how to balance getting the things that will bring you great joy and memories, with things that are just a waste of money that you can save for the future.

It can take a little practice, but once you see the value in your efforts, you will continue saving for your future.

Works Cited

Krantz, Matt. "Many have little to no savings as retirement looms." *USA Today* 4 December 2011.

Coombes, A. (2013, September 17). *Market Watch*. Retrieved September 23, 2013, from Market Watch: http://www.marketwatch.com/story/investors-too-optimistic-for-their-own-good-2013-09-17?link=sfmw

Made in the USA
San Bernardino, CA
06 February 2018